# BLAKE

Angel Rosen

ISBN: 9798424399602

## AND THEN, BLAKE…

Following *Aurelia*, this collection of poems came together as a result of the ongoing battle with my enormity.

These poems contemplate suicide, taking up space, grief, infatuation, neurodiversity, friendship, the expectations of womanhood, and the constant performance of being human.

The concept of *Blake* comes from the song "Blake Says" by Amanda Palmer. To me, *Blake* means defying convention. *Blake* means being loved for being authentic and to love someone's entirety. I have always wanted to be loved like that. Some days, it seems possible that I already am.

I offer that love, and hope that it comes back to me.

# AURELIA

A small girl makes a fist for the first time
only once, and it
never unclenches. This fist
begins to shatter the world,
beginning many faults,
holding a pencil, saying no,
saying no again, and staying angry.

A small girl feels mad for the first time
only once, and she
goes home a thousand times after that.
She folds her arms and wonders
when things become fair,
but all things in the sky
answer *never.*

## ROUND ONE

One night in 2001,
I played *Who Wants to be a Millionaire.*
The one-hundred-dollar question was
"Which month sometimes has twenty-nine days?"

As a first grader, I knew everything.
I exclaim, "I want to phone a friend!"
My aunt Ruth passes me a pink Lisa Frank cell phone
and I dial the numbers.
She plays along and asks who is on the line.

I hold the phone up to my ear
and say "Hi, God?
I'm playing Who Wants to be a Millionaire
and if you answer this one question for me,
I may have a chance at winning.
February sometimes has twenty-nine days, all months do,
my question is, why was I born?"

Laughter is only one letter different from slaughter.
One typo later,
God laughs.
I'm cut in half. Next round.

## MAD GIRL LOVES WRONG

*after "Mad Girl's Love Song" by Sylvia Plath*

I sink myself into the bath,
I have never known myself.
This ache is a play, three acts.

I'm the loser, coming last,
I choose a knife from the shelf.
I sink myself into the bath.

The end is this: the lovers laugh,
I plan a grisly farewell.
This ache is a play, three acts.

When I'm open, she brings a patch.
It's a game of show and tell,
I sink myself into the bath.

Adequate rivals, me and Sylvia Plath—
The Damaged Woman, a jar, a bell.
This ache is a play, three acts.

## ANGELICA AND RUE

Down the stairs, she goes.
She thinks this catastrophe is small enough
to fit into her pocket. Tragedy sighs
its December breath, minty,
full of greed and grinning children.

Every bunch of us is a set
of scraped knees, bright as
red berries. The holly bush surprise:
*Baby shoes. Never worn.*

She shows her dawns so well,
saturated with sunrises and
night sweats that evolve into morning—
the Jekyll and Hyde, pre-menopause, of
a woman adorning the consequences
of another person's violence.

It's a mere inconvenience. She
nibbles on the edges of her
angelica and rue—
there's enough blood in her.
It always comes to a halt,
and with age, a conclusion.

Every man can be sponged off,
this one, with a little extra nudging.
There is a caroler outside—
an odd display for this time of year, but good
practice for all the future's joy.

Her thighs become templates.
The small indents take the color best
as it pools on her in little episodes.
It's a mere inconvenience, pocket-sized.
She turns gray, her breath
weaving into stench and stealing
from the air the same comfort that
shaped her into this
exhibition.

"What a guilty woman,"
they will say.
"So cruel."
They will say that, too.
They will count her abortifacients and
her affairs and do the math—
anything more than one is too many.
She thought that of herself.
*Baby shoes. Never worn.*
Her obituary is an auction, too.

## THE TEMPERATURE OF LOSS

I caught a cold when I
was eight years old, the kind that
follows a funeral and dead
aunts. I caught a shiver then—
death's explanation,
out against the elements,
wearing nothing
of the warming sort.

I caught a cold when I was
small, a desolate chilliness
that doesn't thaw when
sparrows come back in the spring.

Even their squawking can't disturb
my autumnal underneath that
browns and deadens anything with
too much life. My inevitable winters
follow and they stay, they stay.

Each snowy window I have passed
has been my familiar. Something about
this resented heaviness leaves
people indoors, I know.

I think when cancer first
stole someone from me in that way
and my little hands couldn't
hit hard enough at anything
to get me back through to the side before
when the seasons mattered and I was
only cold for half of the year—
That is when I became loss's shape, became
what loss looks like, my body
leaving loss's dents in my mattress as it
pokes me with springs.
Maybe when I'm older,
a spring will leave a hole in me and
I will finally have something warm.

## COST ANALYSIS

What happens if I don't make it?
Does my phone stop ringing?
I don't think anyone has ever called. Although,
I've answered.
Will you remember to turn off the stove for me?
I don't think it's ever been on. Although,
the water has boiled.
I have some things to wrap up.
A Christmas present,
a deposit so this check doesn't bounce.
Can you walk my dog tomorrow?
I get one Zoom call in the afterlife.
Hello, are you there?
Please, tell me how *Grey's Anatomy* ends.

Where will my aches land? I'm serious, what happens?
If I find myself gone, where do you end up?
If my pain redistributes, who gets the most of it?
Hands up! Any volunteers?
What happens if I don't make it?
Will I finally put my phone down
and stop checking my Twitter?
Will someone tell Amanda?
Will you update my away message
on AOL Instant Messenger?

Do I get to bring my straight A report cards
to heaven or wherever I end up?
What do they amount to there?
Can I buy something with them?
Maybe it's like an arcade, the afterlife.
You trade in some of what you have for the chance
to win something else, but none of it's real.
Not the money. Not the prize.
Twenty dollars for a rubber ball,
one hundred tickets for a stuffed giraffe.
I will take both. Spin again. Throw a dart.
I may end up with something beautiful
that is never worth the cost.

## BUYER'S REMORSE

Grief consumes me, grows a face,
changes the channel,
supersizes my Happy Meal,
puts the toy on a shelf,
arrives in a cardboard box to my porch,
gallops.

Grief circles a drain, ties a balloon animal,
posts a controversy on the timeline,
debates the validity of art,
adopts a Neopet.

Grief buys a jacket, leaves it on the back
of a chair at a bar, buys another one,
uploads a new profile picture,
gets an SAT score of 1580,
joins a pyramid scheme,
begs for attention,
deletes evidence,
kills its goldfish,
transmogrifies.

## QUANDARY

all I can say is that
cruelty was leaking out of you
but I had no empty buckets
within arms' reach so I
had to swallow all of it
mouth agape taking in
hundreds of ounces of
such loathsome stuff
turning myself inside out
to scrub at intervals
hoping I could sleep
underneath your ceiling
without it caving in
waking up with
polystyrene between my teeth
your mistake was believing
that I was the one
making the mess
simply because I could not
house all of it
you were spitting so much
contempt
I met my body's limits
and by Sunday I was swollen
with your nonsense and there was
no room for absolutely anything else

## SEARCH RESULTS

I am looking everywhere for you.
I have checked my emails,
the answers on Jeopardy,
the since-abandoned Spirit Halloween,
the hotel in which I was yours for the first time,
the backyard of a friend's childhood home,
in between my folded towels.
You are nowhere
and that's alarming.

I am looking everywhere for you.
I will check
the KFC that used to be an AutoZone,
your aunt's apartment on Google Maps,
the Zen garden you put lines in with a miniature rake,
the chorus of every song I've ever known,
my esophagus,
my DVD collection between *Cujo* and *Cabaret*,
the restaurant down the street.

If I haven't found you in any of those places,
I think I will look in the cow pastures
near my house, the dial tone
when I contemplate typing your number
into my phone's lifeless body,
my mattress at the landfill.

If you are not in the coffee mug
holding several pens,
my neighbor's fire pit,
printed onto a facsimile
without a cover page,
you are nowhere in the office at all.

As a last resort, I will extract
one molar and see
if you are in a root.  I will look for you
under anesthesia.
You are nowhere
and that's alarming.

## ASCENDING AS A LYNX

My mom invented grizzly bears.
There were only twelve at first
until one sat in the sky and became a ladle.
All nursery rhymes are about animals
or the night. This makes a cartoon
of everything frightening.

My mom invented knick-knacks and a place
to put them, I collected every useless thing
that cost her a dollar. My mom invented dollars.

Like a plant eager for sunlight and acknowledgement,
I repot myself; I move from the box of
toy cars and plastic horses to one with buttons,
bouncy balls and quarter machine rings.

I establish myself next to a board game,
eventually into the finger holes of a six-pound bowling ball,
sandwiched between seventh grade math assignments,
into a spool of a VHS tape, flickering, I
leap into carnival-won stuffed animals, attend their
public hanging, acquaint myself
with a dead mouse, sew my baby teeth
to the back of my neck, take
ibuprofen, invent the wheel.

I put myself in bubble wrap, ask for
an extension, tiptoe into a canyon of mugs,
stickers, cat figurines, one special marble,
crayons. I can't find the one thing I am looking for
in here, I move the insulation out of the skylight,
use a knife to peel off the wall, reveal mold, I leave it all
disheveled and try to feed myself to the bear in the sky.
I ascend and become the lynx.

## SIMULACRUM

My kite's been situated.
I am at the mercy of the sky,
saturnine thing.
Ribbon-tailed and playing sting-ray.
Apotheosis, but still paltry.
No matter all the ways in which
I am above, I am not the God
you seek. In just a minute,
any gull or pull could bring me down.

Unfortunately bright and regrettably aerial,
you see me first but do not pray to me—
Impressive for this breezy day above saltwater,
impressive for any five-year-old looking up,
but I would be a meager God
if you pray to me. The gales loom.
I am not the symbol you seek.
You would just happen to notice
anything as tall and
as misplaced as me.

## AN EVALUATION OF MY HANDS

When everything comes out at once,
I evaluate my hands. They're so
dumb. I have never caught anything.
I barely carry it. I try to find a place
to put it but I am too crowded.
Nothing fits inside.
I hold a glass plate with a believable grip,
because shattering
is a noise I hate more than
responsibility. Bloody noses
over sinks. I've survived repairs.
I traded my serotonin for a day's
worth of horror.
I came star-studded for every premiere, every film,
I am the suicide in all of them.
It's usually right before the end.
Don't change the channel.
When everything comes out at once,
I evaluate my script. It's so
dumb. I have never

## ANCHOR

I am something that you get stuck with
like the ghost of the noose you tied at sixteen.

The Adderall and the surface cuts
were no longer scene-stealers,
your yawning audience of teachers,
parents, and equally anorexic friends,
casually waiting for the opening act
of you to conclude,
while you wake up again bitter and sober,
they thumb through their playbills in the dark.

Typecast as the girl feigning a Lazarus injury,
dying but still posting on Facebook,
another diagnosis
could explain this better.

I am your damned childhood friend
who was with you in the accident,
a decade of revisiting our intactness together,
accounting for each other, tattooed. I am your
best setback and most ceaseless reminder,
the biggest scar you wear is the one I've
sunken into with you.

You steady—walk the plank, walk the tight-rope,
walk at all, walk the straight line
back to your vehicle, and you leave. The wound
I lie in nudges at my dead-bed.
Who says you get to leave?
On your way out, I tighten and sway,
catching you in the door,
a red scarf for our final embrace—
stuck, stuck, stuck.

## CUMBERSOME

It takes much more time now to leave the house.
While you recite "phone, wallet, keys," I check
to make sure I have hand lotion, a sense of humor,
and someone who loves me. Sometimes I don't have two
of those and while I put lotion on my hands for
the twentieth time today, I wonder if
I could just turn around now and stay inside.
I can't possibly take everything with me.
I am already a spectacle, can you imagine
the ridiculous woman who packs her house in her backpack
to make sure she can be comfortable anywhere else
for one or more hours?
When I am out, people ask me "What's wrong?"
I'd love to answer, but I can't tell them the truth.
I left my house at home, but at least I packed my mints.
"Nothing, just tired,"
I say, although true, it's an understatement.
For life, I have come, overpacked.

## A RECIPE FOR A BIRTHDAY

1. An age: reluctantly announced
2. Several friends: but not enough
3. A cake: that you'll eventually throw up
4. A necklace: you'll never wear
5. A laugh: in unison

Choose a room, one larger than the number of people you know.

Assort your people based upon how well you know them.

Serve them cake for about 20 minutes (at least one person will decline).

Quietly tell them they should have left their diet at home.

Open a gift, pretend you don't already have it,

shuffle your friends and hope that the joker lands on top.

Somebody cheers!

They are aware that you survived something.

Take several photos, at least one with a smile.

Post them one day later.

Accept birthday wishes for the next five business days.

Contemplate all of the birthday cards relatives forgot

to send you twelve years ago

and where those cards went when they died.

Everybody sings

or something.

## ON THE RECORD

Your honor,
I am not responsible for
the centipedes in the sink,
your lost dry cleaning,
third divorce or sixth guilty verdict.

No one here is any good at fencing
but they would rather fence
than be jurors.

Your honor,
I am not responsible for
the lost marbles,
the clogged drain
or the guts on the rug.

The second juror from the left
is looking rather handsome
in this fluorescent light.

Your honor,
I am not responsible for
my unshaven legs,
tipped kayak
or your morning fender bender.

Please grant me house arrest
and the grounds for an appeal.
Hold me in contempt,
hold me at all.

Your honor,
I am not responsible for
the long line at the McDonald's,
your cold coffee,
your daughter's loser boyfriend or my
disproportionate reaction to nearly everything.
Sometimes I say one thing
and do another, but
I am not responsible for that.

## MELANCHOLY

It's another year and I still wonder if
you think I'm funny.
I still kill everything I plant.
I keep the dog alive,
I feed the neighbor's cat ironically.
You used to laugh and say "you're strange,"
I was so proud to be both this odd and yours.
It's not so different. Some days I remember
to close the refrigerator door,
other days, things spoil. If you were here
maybe you would joke with me
about all the food we buy
and never eat. I'd laugh despite my guilt.

You took her to the museum and said
she was everything in it. Suddenly,
I am so heedless in my one-woman show
as the brazen, unlovable fool, who once
had a love that looked over her shoulders
as she washed the dishes. A love that
noticed when the sky looked like cotton candy
and when it was more orange cream.

I think you were tired of balancing. Some days,
I'd hand you my spoons and cereal boxes.

You used to understand why it was
that we must always pack the kitchen.
You were much more mindful of your pots,
where tea was lovingly poured from,
and how you'd die if one were to shatter. I thought
oh, to be a kettle, to be a pot. I would love to be
the handle you sought for warmth again, but like you
with me, I carelessly let each one hit the tile.
We didn't pack the kitchen that day. In shambles and sugar,
not even kintsugi could make us whole or beautiful again.
You suggested you'd had enough of my
gold and fairytales, I ran my fingers through your hair
and it turned to straw. You laughed but not with me,
at your own disassembly. I used to humor you,
and then I aged you, I stayed sanguine,
you grew melancholy.
It was the only thing that grew in our house.

## PIROUETTE

This moving picture:
tattoo graffiti,
a body, a body.
Well-practiced ballerina,
everything coming to a point,
he ends and begins in a line.

His swiftness,
such nectar for the eyes.
Tiny dancers aligned,
*Maestro,* all rise!
This cosmic confection
is coming to its final act.
There is always a bow
and standing ovations
but the act is something
poorly aged.

The velveteen boy,
the opus, ego-stroked-goldness,
leotard and tights,
perfect architect angles,
it's all a recording
until the end.

Piano—flute—violin—
Pierrot the clown,
the final arabesque,
a lightning assemblé
the music, a merciless error,
all assume.

The barrel growls,
a copper-plated end,
the clown concludes,
no applause.
He begins and ends in a line.

## INGREDIENTS

Is your woman made of glass?
If you put your hand through her,
do you bleed out with shards of her
in your wrist? Perhaps a window
to look out and see your luxury,
or a decanter from which
you drink your death.
Is your woman made of wood?
If you slice her and peel off the bark,
do you have a set of stools
for all of your drunk friends?
Perhaps best paired with a table
made out of your first wife.
Is your woman made of silver?
Is she the world's best conduit,
making a socket or a locket
equally dangerous for your hands?
A thoughtful gift if boxed
and included with a portrait
in a matching silver frame.
Is your woman made of mint?
Does she pair with mojitos and lamb?
Does she freshen the back of your throat?
Green in this life, a mild astringent.
There is no right answer. You should
crumple up your list of ingredients.

## THE DISCARD

You exhaust me first thing
when I wake up.
I tighten your screws,
you lay me back down
and beg for me to be useless
but I have so many uses.
I pour your drinks,
I justify your thirst in the first place.
I pour the fabric softener,
I justify the blankets in the bed
in the first place.

I wash a dish
yes, I'm your bitch,
someday I will leave them
stacked up high beside the
sink, just like your
misery at our bedside.
Someday, I will leave the grease
to eat through the
plates and your
misery through you.

## MY DEPARTURE

I have a train of thought,
I announce its arrival at 8:30 p.m.
until it veers slightly to the right
onto someone else's forearm
where it lands or something similar.

No one has ever hacked
away at themselves in my absence, but
I dream of nothing less horrible than that.
Everything pending eventually
dissolves into a decision, I am
the cruel result of that inevitability.
I am thinking it is time to be final.
Now, a wagtail makes a stage of my fist,
and for the first and last time,
my daughter believes in miracles.

We picked up a stray dog. She names it Josie,
we're not keeping it but I have invited
this miracle into Thursday. She asks for a sleepover.
I consult the bird for its conscience.
The dog gets the bottom bunk, my daughter
gets one more good day, my
septum ring rusts in my nose as I cry myself
to sleep, hugging my empty womb, wishing
she could go with me.

Pain borrows my husband's mouth and says
*single file,* pain says
*the next bus comes at ten o'clock,*
*it's the last one for the week,*
*holiday schedule.*
I unfold my last night's sleep
and pour it into a half-empty syrup bottle.
Her morning will still come
and she will still want breakfast.

## PURGE CONDITIONS

The last time I purged
which was Wednesday this week,
the rest of what I had to say
went down with the
breakfast cake. Cake for
breakfast, battery acid for lunch,
an epiphany follows and I'm
reluctantly full again by 5:00 p.m.
*Le rendez-vous du soir,*
I hate everyone I've ever
loved for insisting I was inedible
and I wonder if I ration
all the hypotheticals, if someday,
they can go down with the flush.
If purging could actually make me
empty instead of giving
them more space to rattle,
I would never let anything
stay down. My intestines would
become idle corridors. I would be
the theory of thinness but
without the result—I do not
want to be small as in thin, I just want
to be filled with a less volatile stuffing,
but doomed finales
do not exit from the mouth.

## HEDWIG SYNDROME

The bright boy is made of crystal and cigarettes,
with a line of tally marks down his arm
to write his prescriptions in.
He's been more brilliant than the sun since he was ten.
Illuminating everything, drying it out.
In an eighth-grade study hall, I tried to draw a
perfect friend, and it always looked like him.

He has his head in the oven beside mine.
A case of Hedwig Syndrome.
It's how we met—both of us had this fate with different
endings. At fifteen, he gave me a box full of musicians.
He would say
*Angel, I wish I was dead, but until then, we can listen to Placebo.*
We barely survived this youth, but it had a good soundtrack.
My bright boy, my New Year's Eve companion,
living room tattoos, the MySpace trendsetter,
the walk in a blizzard for Newports,
French class, The Dresden Dolls,
driver's ed and me never learning to drive.
Drag in the daytime, piano at night, background music
for all of the best times we endured alongside the laundromat,
to end up in an apartment full of misfits.
He's pink on the inside, every inch of him angry,
but what a masterpiece, this love.
*Après moi*, now comes the blood.

## HORSE BOY

Sometimes, I imagine myself as a drawing,
erasable in the same way.
On paper, you can crumple me up, burn me,
throw me in the trash.
I can delete myself. I don't have to wait
for you to do it. It's just two clicks.
I befriend an artist
just to say that I know someone.
I watch over his shoulder in envy.
He turns a stop sign into a grapefruit.

Sometimes, I hear hooves.
I always think *zebras.* I call a zookeeper.
She puts me on hold and says to the receptionist,
"It's just her again, horse girl."
They never believe me. One day, I let
the zebras out. I don't have to wait
for you to do it for me. It's just two clicks.
I hear hooves, I call no one and take a picture.
Headline reads: Zebras!
I sell them my photograph.

Sometimes, I see finish lines.
I never cross them, I think
*slow and steady wins the race.*
I cheer while everyone passes.

One day, he asks why I'm standing
still. I say "I'm not good at anything."
He opens the gate and tells me
to run. I almost make it.

Victor says that I'll be okay.
He doesn't bet on losing horses.

## LOOP

Imagine a photograph
of the hole I emulate, a socket.
Toothpaste stains on my sweatshirt,
I floss intermittently,
brush for seventy seconds,
not long enough, spit,
the dentist says *all good, kid,*
I drink Diet Mountain Dew
once a month, never
eat a lollipop or wait at a stop light
for the cow to cross the highway,
I call the farmer, they come in threes,
at the library, I whisper to someone,
ask, *where's the Lysol?* They hand it to me
in a syringe.

No one coughs or stirs,
I learn to knit, place cashmere
over my rot. I read a chapter book,
two hundred pages. If no one dies
in the book, it's for children,
if everyone dies, it's for teenagers.

I have been sixteen for eleven years.

## WORSHIP

I want you on the other end of all of my best sentences,
I want you on the other side of every dinner table,
I want you between my legs and between my lungs,
in a way that makes us merged and nearly deplorable
I want to look into the mirror and first see
who you love and second who I am, my identity
an embellishment to the body I have given to you
I want Sundays to be our day of worship, my forgiveness
thrown out on our bedsheets instead of in the pews
my tithing given in inches and inspections
my holy water, down my legs in search of you,
take this body / my daily bread / your hymns
are humming / in my head / I am neatly offering you
my empty, uncut palms
so you can nail them to your tongue

## INCREMENTS

On a silver spoon, I will
give you my inches—
just one at a time. I am
better in increments.
Awfully metric.

So many things are deep!
Me, for example—
tight, but not shallow,
the one cut the one time
in that single instance!
Will you explore me?
I am all avenues. Take a map.

When I come out…
into whose mouth?
What will you wash me down with?
You stay content living in my belly,
with your compass and
a little flint, cashews to nourish you,
but I've no water to cure
the saltiness of your tongue.

I have never been full despite the bingeing.
While I cure my hunger, life invents another pit
that grumbles from its mouth.

Oh well. You will take me, right?
You're assessing my size, they always do,
it's ugly on the outside, but I
can fold up real neat!
One inch at a time, for you!

## COORDINATION

The cement gently grazes my knees
as I fall up the stairs again,
carrying a bicycle
I will never learn to ride.
My legs become knotted ribbons,
a fanfare flow art of my idiot limbs.
I scrape my shins every time I make this climb,
it's only five stairs but it's the endeavor.
When I descend, I know I'm risking bee stings
and stepping on cracks
and I think today could really be the day
that I master two wheels and a balancing act.
When I return, sunken with defeat,
the five stairs between being foolish
and going home feel too tall.
I'm a marvelous autistic unacrobat.
My lumbering assault on agility.
He won't take the training wheels off.
The bike and the gate lock rust,
I hear crickets in the rhubarb,
but I know they're not cheering for me.
I have the video tapes to prove I grew up
but I still have two extra wheels
keeping me from bloody elbows and chipped teeth.
I have a list of absences: swimming lessons,
gym class, every school dance and talent show.

I stayed home so that
the contagious humiliation wouldn't
follow me back and never leave.
The time I spent across cement was always brutal.
Through the sophisticated acts of independence:
cartwheels I never mastered,
the impossible choreography of romance,
the stumbling succession of aged-out friendships.
Anything that moves and I are enemies,
I am excellent at being still, and
even in the most profound stillness—
I have had to keep the helmet on.

## A DIFFERENT FIG

She is every woman
and so elongated are the days that are fitting
months inside them, seeping,
asking for the audience
and for the pity of motherhood
to collapse just as neat.
Come get your girl!

She is made of Paris and ashes,
she is a fine cuisine
and the sizzle of its birth.
A bouquet of roses,
at least, for every time
a loved one bears a child
and we record that daughter's
first defeat in ounces and inches.

She is a romantic
on the heels of someone
much taller than her
when she kisses
another person's fabrications
to solidify the hideous promise
of forever and its short-lived phenomenon.

In the morning,
there is a fried egg and jam
and none of the proper utensils,
but they make the noises
of any other breakfast.
Come get your girl!

The crib is so disappointing.
A basket of sons caterwauling
because no such thing soothes them,
no extravagant girl, no sweet puree,
no hummed lullaby.

She fancied the screaming men
for her familiar dreams.
A Bible under her pillow,
the discussion.
Body half in an ambulance,
the other half giving a lecture
to another set of sons.

What a brilliant despair
neatly spun and
depicted as motherhood.
A jamboree of ill-convincing.
Why is she like that?

Threadbare and vile to the nines,
she stirs her blaming pot.
The children and their kerfuffles,
their napkins and plastic keys.
This was too ambitious,
this womanhood and the commitments of
care and nurture.

She will try a different one next time,
her hands more delicately choosing
a different fig from the tree.

## HYSTERIA CYCLE

It has been thirty-two days, and my world is ending again.
Death? I know it, it has had its snout pressed against my face.
I have felt its hot air coming out either side,
making fog. Eye to eye. Satan, come get your
shepherd's hound. I am tired of the growling,
all this noise but no sweet release, no beast
embedded in my neck. It seems like
a lot of fuss for nothing. I do not get to die.

There will be a parade for that later.
For now, I am merely death's obstacle.
What a face he has! He frightens the paperboys,
they shall accept no news.
They keep this bastard on a leash.
I wish my sickness was quadrupedal.
I wish it would slip its collar,
a noose with a jingle bell.

I hear the clink and the footsteps,
all sounds mimic applause.
I am waiting for the news to come:
Will she make it? Will she make it?
What are the odds! I do not get to die.
Time for your parade.
Excuse me, though, I must be brave
in another room. There are claws there, too.

## WHAT WILL YOU HAVE?

*I've never been to Starbucks,* I say,
sinking. I hate coffee.
I am having an affair with being the contrary.
You think poetry starts in the morning with brown liquid,
stench of newspaper, hum of talk radio,
a call from a friend of the past, an irony.

I think poetry starts an hour after
I said I would sleep, but my hands travel.
The liquids are undeniably red,
Easter egg dye sitting on my right thigh,
little threads of skin lay in my thimble untied,
stench of citrus, hum of television,
mindless until all that is the mind.

When you are ten and you spin,
dizzy is something you're warned about, you fall,
you laugh, you tell anyone about your bruise
for a day until you find the next news story
on your body. When you are ten and you
lay upside down, the blood rushes to your head,
an aunt insists you stop.
I wondered if the blood has to stay inside.
I cut my thumb with
a razor in a box on an old wooden stair,
I panicked and then reported.

It wasn't front-page. Stench of
coffee, newspaper sans my scoop,
sans me at all, I lay upside down,
not ten, the blood rushes,
I get to know it, say,
*I hate coffee, what else do you have?*
Oh, plenty, but it's full price
even with the glass half empty.

## IN THIS ACT, I DIE FIRST

Sweet Cupid, I have a knot
in my stomach the shape of your
inadequacies; kiss me badly,
make summer stick to my bedsheets
and my wide belly. Feed me Pepto Bismol.
I am not going to get better this time.
Hammer and nail,
all resources arriving, tick away
at my years, chisel
until it's all debris in a landslide and a too-long
episode of a hit TV show
knowing my end, staying relevant. I want
to be talked about, so I must be first,
Romeo. Eating the soupy details
with a fork, you get
almost none of it,
you're just stirring and I go regardless.

## SUGARWOOD

The living room door
in my aunt Margaret's house
had the face of Jesus in the grain.
When I would fall asleep
with its eyes watching me
I thought I would wake up healed—
salvation on the other side
of sugarwood.

When I was three, I remember
my mother carrying me
because our street had flooded
and I said
"I thought you told me
God would never flood the earth again?"
Turns out, my town wasn't the whole world.

I took up my grievance
with the door.
With my little hands, I unscrewed
the hinges and offered
it to Noah for an arc.

## THE HOUDINI SHADOW

For years, I've had a shadow that barks.
Sometimes it sneezes or howls.
These noises are my favorite song.
No matter where I go,
this shadow follows me,
bringing its love.
The sound of this love is sometimes
claws tapping on a hardwood floor,
it's the sound of drinking
water out of a bowl at night.
Despite our imperfections,
a dog's love has no condition.
They have all of our humanity
with none of the cruelty.
They just want to follow you,
live in your shadow,
and be loved back.

For years, I've had a shadow
that I feed two times a day,
that I walk on a leash,
that I tuck into bed,
that I keep warm,
and hug close when it thunders loudly.
I kiss his pink tongue.
He trusts me. Together, we are safe.

## BLAKE

Blake says not much for certain,
leaving text messages unread,
opening only boxes that contain
a circumstance that he must tend to.
Something to be busy about.
Blake says less now, nods at
animals he passes by, smiles
at the people on the street.

Blake goes more than not,
away but never further,
a seraph aching to be sure,
folds his wings down into a
case to finally be an angel all the time.

# NOTES & ACKNOWLEDGEMENTS

Cover Illustration by Victor Carlesi.

"Mad Girl Loves Wrong" follows Sylvia Plath's "Mad Girl's Love Song" and "A Different Fig" gets its inspiration from Plath's *The Bell Jar.* "Blake" follows the song *Blake Says* by Amanda Palmer.

"A Recipe for a Birthday" was originally published in *The 2020 Poetry Marathon Anthology.* "Sugarwood" was originally published in *The 2021 Poetry Marathon Anthology.*

I dedicate this book to my beloved dogs:
Houdini, Doodle (Benson), Hollywood, Calvin and Beaker.

I want to express my gratitude for Amanda Palmer who has been a constant source of inspiration and love in my life since I was fifteen.

I want to thank Victor for supporting me endlessly and helping me survive the last five years. His friendship has inspired me to grow in ways I didn't know were possible.

I also want to give a special thanks to my friends, Joshua and Megan, for helping me during my editing process with this book. I am grateful for all of the love and support of my friends and online communities which made this book possible. Thank you for reading, listening, understanding, and giving my art a reason to exist.

# ABOUT THE AUTHOR

*Still bigger than anyone lovable.*

When people tell you that you're too much that sometimes means that you're a woman, queer, fat, or neurodivergent. That's too many things to be and I am all of them.

I'm just a person tweeting my grief into the universe and then formatting it into a book.

I've been writing since third grade. The first poem I ever wrote down was about a blue cow. Since then, I have written constantly about every ache and every joy I've endured. Whenever I'm not writing… I'm reading, tweeting, texting, psychoanalyzing someone, or pressing "next episode" on whatever series I'm currently watching. Sometimes, I even leave the house.

I am a poet first before anything else.

Find more about my poetry and life at angelrosen.com.

Made in the USA
Las Vegas, NV
13 May 2022

48858682R00038